The Food Truck Business Book

A Step-By-Step Guide for Beginners to Start and Grow a Successful Mobile Food Business

By

Pier Fuller

Disclaimer

This publication is designed to provide competent and reliable information regarding the subject matter covered. However, the views expressed in this publication are those of the author alone, and should not be taken as expert instruction or professional advice. The reader is responsible for his or her own actions.

The author hereby disclaims any responsibility or liability whatsoever that is incurred from the use or application of the contents of this publication by the purchaser or reader. The purchaser or reader is hereby responsible for his or her own actions.

Table of Contents

Introduction 7

Chapter 1 9

The Basics of Food Truck 9

  Food Trucking History 9

  Advantages and Disadvantages 12

  Food Truck Owner Routine..................................... 16

Chapter 2 21

Getting Started... 21

  How to Name Your Food Truck 21

  Cost of Running a Food Trucking Business 26

  How to Finance Your Food Truck Business................ 31

  Deciding on The Location of Your Food Truck 39

    Street Parking 40
    Food Truck Parks 40
    Business Districts and Large Office Buildings............. 41
    Farmers Markets 42
    Bars and Clubs.. 42

Festivals, Events, and Sports Venues 43

Gas Stations 43

College Campuses 43

Food Menu and Pricing 45

Chapter 3 58

Business Plan Development 58

Chapter 4 67

The Rules and Regulations 67

Establish The Structure of Your Business 67

Obtain Your EIN 69

Get The Necessary Permits and Licenses 69

Insure Your Food Truck 73

Zoning and Parking Restrictions 75

Chapter 5 76

Getting Your Food Truck 76

Available Options For a Food Truck 76

Do This Before Selecting a Truck 77

Chapter 6 84

Designing Your Food Truck 84

Selecting The Right Vehicle 84

Running Your Food Truck 86

Food Truck Layout 88

Food Truck Mobility 91

Food Truck Branding 94

Food Truck Bathrooms 95

Chapter 7 97

Food Truck Supplies and Equipment 97

Chapter 8 103

Procedures For Food Safety 103

Chapter 9 107

Hiring and Managing Your Team 107

Chapter 10 112

Advertising Your Food Truck Business 112

Chapter 11 126

Food Truck Mistakes to Avoid 126

Conclusion 131

Introduction

Years ago, a man named Charles Goodnight was the first to invent a mobile food business idea very similar to a food truck. But then, this idea was picked up by several others who then transformed it into what it is know as today, food truck, which operates in its tens of thousands across the US.

The food trucking business is not one to jump right into without first understanding what it takes to own and operate a food truck. There are several laws, regulations, and principles guiding the operation of a food truck business that you must adhere to if you want to succeed with minimal issues of course. You also want to ensure that you are making the right decisions and applying the right strategies to get you your desired result. Laying hold of these insider secrets to jumpstart your food trucking business into success might prove difficult except you have privy access to the right knowledge and resources. However, congratulations because you are in the right place to access lots of invaluable nuggets that will take you from ground zero right into running a successful food truck business.

Without much ado, let's jump right into the first chapter to get you started.

Chapter 1

The Basics of Food Truck

Food Trucking History

The History of the Food Truck began in the year 1866. And all the acknowledgments tied to the birth of such wonderful invention are attributed to Texas Panhandle's patron, Charles Goodnight. Charles was known as one of the experts known to have handled the system of ranching, and he had several attributes tied to him. He was said to be bright, and cheery, along with a record of being an ardent smoker that fiddled with more than fifty cigarettes a day. Another very interesting thing about Charles was that he married a twenty-six-year-old woman, who worked as a nurse when he was ninety-one. Shocking, yes? These things contributed a lot to him being very famous in Texas, but then, asides from all of that, he managed to craft the very best of the inventions still used today by many, both in Texas and in the world at large.

What exactly is this Food Truck, and how did Charles manage to get it into the minds of people? Why was it the talk of the town? And why should you even bother to get yourself acquainted with it?

The Food truck was designed as a mobile kitchen. When Charles Goodnight initially developed the idea, it was because of his cattle. Funny, you might think, but indeed, that was the plan. He had to embark on a long trip, and because he wasn't opportune to travel along the rails, he'd constructed a wagon that was quite analogous to the one used in the army. He'd equipped the wagon with everything he needed, right from shelves to water barrels to compartments for firewood. If we were to talk about how he managed not to starve, we'd discover how he brought along with him everything he could think of, right from dried beans to corn to chunks of salted meat. The rest, he gathered, as he traveled.

A few other people began to build on Charles' idea, and the first person we'd reckon with here is Walter Scott. He was the one who constructed the first stand for food, where he sold pie and coffee to journalists who never really had time for breakfast. His food stand was constructed with a wagon as the very foundation, and just by the sides, he cut out squares for windows, and rectangles for doors. It came out beautiful and several other people thought to make something similar to what he'd done.

In 1984, more of these food structures were erected in the campuses of the Ivy League, and there, sausages were sold to the college kids that schooled there. Later on, in 1936, the first cart where hot dogs were sold was erected, and it was spotted with wheels that made it mobile, unlike the older creations. In 1950, the trucks were then used to sell ice cream and other frozen treats. So, really, over the years, food trucks have faced tons of improvements, but technology-wise and industrial-wise. And most importantly, several people love the whole idea of it and have stuck to using it to build their businesses.

Indeed, right now, the food truck business has grown so wide that you would notice it in the figures—there are over four thousand of it in the U.S. And several people—about thirteen thousand—have been able to make a means of livelihood out of it. Today, the food truck business industry has a net worth of approximately one billion dollars, which is certainly worth everything Charles Goodnight began.

Advantages and Disadvantages

Knowing the good and the bad in running a food truck comes as one very crucial requirement before you begin this business. Those extra details will help you to know the good things that a food truck will bring to you. It will also go a long way to help you maximize your potential profits and other factors. And then, a knowledge of its shortcomings would also help you know if this is really what you want.

Advantages

1. You get to make your menu: The food trucking business is essential for those who have one or two culinary skills from which they want to make some money. Now, the amazing thing is that a food truck comes as a mini restaurant that is very possible to be managed all by oneself. And that sole proprietorship gives you the grace to craft out your dishes and menu. So, this idea is great if you have that recipe that you've secretly worked on at home. No doubt, everyone would not mind having a taste of the food items you have on your menu.

2. You can be your boss: Having to work under some other person can be frustrating, as you'd be forced to channel your creativity, time, and paycheck to whatever your employer demands. However, with the food truck, you've got it all in control. You could decide to do anything however you like, place anything anywhere, and really, that is the exact definition of freedom. In the long run, you end up spending more time building up your establishment and making cool cash because you are happy.

3. There are lesser risks compared to you opening an actual restaurant: Building a restaurant or acquiring a building for the major aim of offering food to the public can present a whole lot of risks to the table. It requires that you invest more money, time, and strategies, just to see that a positive result is achieved by you. However, with a food truck business, you can cut through a whole lot of that stress. Most of the chefs today start small with the food truck business, and then, later on, move on to running actual restaurants. Either way, a food truck will make you ready for

whatever risks may be on the way. It's small and quite easy to manage.

4. You get a thousand opportunities to actively engage: The beauty of a food trucking business lies greatly in its mobility. You don't have to sit in some building and then, wait for your customers to find you. You could turn the tables around and then, search out your customers. All you just need to do is locate the places with the potential for the best sales, and then, sell to them. A few of these places include parks, festivals, and areas where employees of a company relax during their break. This way, you get to promote your food trucking business and also reach out to as many customers as possible.

Disadvantages

1. You might have to get used to working in confined compartments: Food trucking businesss really would not offer you as much space as actual buildings would. It even gets worse when you add in the necessary equipment and other utensils. So, one thing you might have to adjust to is the small space. Usually, all you get most times

is nothing larger than ten inches by twelve inches truck. So, this might not work out for individuals under the effect of claustrophobia.

2. You must obey the local zoning laws: Several laws guide the operation of food trucks in a particular geographical area, and, to stay in business, you will have to follow every single one of these rules. For example, the fact that a food truck is relatively mobile doesn't give you the grace to just have it parked anywhere. You still have to obey the rules, and regulations that control the zones. So, most times, you might need to plan out your schedule in advance so that you can get a permit to sell wherever you desire. Some other zones also demand that a food truck doesn't park at the same spot two days at a stretch. To be on the safe side, you should make sure to reserve some extra money, as you might have to pay before parking your trucks in a place.

3. You might need to save up for future repairs: Another downside to this business is that it is run in a vehicle. Vehicles could get damaged at any time, and usually, when they do, it'd require that you spend a lot of money in seeing to it that they

are repaired. This issue usually arises when someone who plans on running a food trucking business cannot afford a new food truck. The price of new food trucks falls within the range of $30,000 to about $100,000. So, because of that reason, they opt for older ones which they have to spend a lot of money on just to get them in shape.

4. There's very intense competition in the industry of food trucking: Before you begin this business, take note of the fact that it comes as a very competitive business. There's usually a high demand for cheap meals that would leave the customers coming back for more, so, you have to be sure you can meet up to that challenge. To solve this issue, you just have to think of a way you can stand out from the other food truck businesses. And that would need you to employ a lot of your creativity.

Food Truck Owner Routine

This is the area where we discuss your life as the owner of a food trucking business Indeed, it is not too much of an easy job to be one, as you are practically in charge of everything—repairing the vehicle, crafting out amazing menus, planning where to park your truck, getting the ingredients ready, and several other equally stressful options. As the owner, it is no doubt that you would be the one person spending more time working. We will run through a guide on how your day will turn out the moment you begin this journey.

P.S: A variation in schedule can occur depending on the kind of service you want to work with—breakfast or lunch.

9a.m to 12p.m.

This time range is the period where you hear your alarm goes off, and then, next thing, you are jumping out of your bed in readiness for the new day. Some others could get out of the bed by nine a.m., and you could too, and again, that depends on the kind of schedule you take on for yourself. The next couple hours are what you would spend doing your early morning activities, and planning your day. When handling a business where you have people you work with, you'd probably have a fixed time at which you meet to discuss the things you have in store for the day. Then, from there, you drive up to whichever location is good for selling your food.

12p.m to 12.30p.m

This should be the time where you gather together with your teammates to discuss new ideas, plans, strategies, and the lessons that were picked up from the previous day. Discussing your plans and new strategies, for example, will go a long way in keeping things running smoothly. Doing this would help you come up with the best plans, and most importantly, jeer you up for the day's work.

12.30p.m to 5.30p.m

This time range is the time where you get all the ingredients for the day ready. Sometimes, you could resort to purchasing them that day, for quality and freshness. Some other times, the ingredients could have been purchased a day before. It all depends on the kind of ingredients making up your menu items. Once that is done, you want to move to chop whatever needs to be chopped. This time range is also the perfect time to grill your meat slices till they turn golden. So, you could call this the time to prepare.

It is also very sensible to have with you people who aren't actively involved in the preparation of food. What these do is manage your social media accounts to notify your customers and several others about your new recipes, and promo sales. These people would also be effective in helping you make the necessary calls if orders and deliveries are included in the services you offer. So, this is the time where they function actively too.

5.30p.m to 6p.m

This time range describes the period where you go ahead to wrap up the day's work. You then drive away from the park to the original location of your truck.

6p.m to 2.30a.m

This time range describes the period where you do everything that the owner of a business should do—the thinking, the planning, the strategy development, the calculations, and every other thing. Usually, the hours you spend doing this depend on how much you want to see your business grow and thrive, among the several food trucking businesses in a particular location. You bring your creativity to life, and then, trying things to improve upon the next day. You could also try out a few more recipes, or watch a couple of other videos that would help you brush up on your skills. This is also the time where you see to it that you starting up a food trucking business is the right thing. You'd want to check out your records to see that you are making profit, and meeting your daily goals.

2.30p.m to 5a.m

Now, it is time to head back to business. This time range is defined by you cleaning your truck, and then, making it ready for the next day's work. If there's a need to have something preordered, this time range is the best for that.

P.S: You should also ensure that in doing all of these things, that you take out a couple of hours to eat, and keep your body and your mind in one piece. You could also take a day off when you begin to feel the ugly effects of stress. You need not worry about the breaks though, as it would only help you get more creative. Remember, the best ideas are gotten when you have yourself subjected to leisure's arms.

Chapter 2

Getting Started

Now, having had a good grab on what a food truck business is, and have decided that it is indeed what you desire to get involved in, you can now move on to the next stage, which involves you getting started on how to properly start up a food truck business. How can you kick off your plans as a first-timer? What are the things you need to think of? And yes, what are the things you need to get? Here, we will be discussing all these points altogether.

How to Name Your Food Truck

The first thing you want to think of after deciding that you want to start a food truck business is the name you want to give it. Every business has to have a name, and really, you might need to get creative to bring it to the forefront of your desired customers. You want something that would make them check your hand-outs twice or maybe thrice, and then, buy from you when you finally begin. In choosing the right name for your food trucking business, we would look at all the tips you might probably need.

1. There is a need for you to decide on what it is that you want to sell: Coming up with a name is the first thing you should do to make people aware of whatever it is you are selling. So, at first glance, they can tell if it's pizza or ice cream. That would be a very good catch for you as a newbie in the food trucking business. For example, a name like 'The pizza hut' is clear enough to acquaint your customers with the fact that you sell pizzas. So, simply start with a name that is clear and descriptive enough.

2. Make the name something your target buyers can hardly ever forget: A catchy name is a catch for a new food truck owner. You want something that would keep on ringing in their minds until they eventually give in to their desires to taste your menu items. This is where every bit of your creativity would come out being very useful.

3. Make it a priority to up with a name that people can easily pronounce: To solve this issue, come up with a name that you can pronounce. The keyword being 'you.' If you can't pronounce it, then, there's little possibility of your customers being able to.

4. Avoid being vague when informing the public on what it is you want to sell: This tip comes in handy when there are several varieties of whatever it is you are offering to your clients. One question that you should ask of yourself is this—when you plan on making dishes, do you want to settle on either local or international dishes? Ensure that whatever choice you come up with is clear to your customers.

5. If you are offering a variety of foods to your customers, ensure that you cover a wide range of options: Having a name like 'confectionary' store in a scenario where you are offering more products than confectionaries wouldn't exactly tell your consumers what it is that you supply. So, see to it that you paint a general picture in their minds.

6. Keep the name short and catchy: Long names that would only lead to your customer's tongues getting tied are definitely what you want to avoid as you begin your journey as the owner of a food trucking business. You have to make it a crucial point to stick with something simple enough that

would roll off the tongue easily. For the best effect, stick with just three words.

7. Stay away from controversial names: Avoid names that would stir up controversies among your customers. Even if a name sounds nice to you, there's every possibility that it sounds offensive to another.

8. Ensure that the name you come up with isn't already registered: It can be very bad to tag your business with some name that has been registered by someone else. That would only lead to legal issues which will only end up destroying all of your hard work. If you stay in the United Kingdom, you can check to see if the name you choose for your business has already been taken on the Companies House. For those in the US, you can check the United States Patent and Trademark Office. You could also check your local government site for entity name check tools.

9. Name of food plus co: The word, 'Co' is something you add to your business name when there are several other people actively involved with your trucking business. The attached word also helps your business seem more professional.

10. Seek the help of those that are close to you—
friends and family: Having the people close to
you fetch you names for your business can
effectively go a long way. And that is because of
their amazing ability to help you with a brilliant
and catchy name.

11. Use words whose vocabulary you are sure of: The
issue most people make here is seen in a situation
where they try merging two words in a bid to
create a sensational name. E.g., tastylish—gotten
from the words, tasty and delicious.

12. List out the names you could use for your
business: You can come up with as many as a
hundred names from which you can choose at the
end of the day. Later on, you can streamline the
list to about ten, and thereafter, your final choice.

13. Being able to conduct a survey online by getting
people to choose which of your name choices
sounds the most appealing.

14. Stay away from names that have geographical
locations tied to them: This reason is that you
might at one time or the other decide to expand
your business to some other location.

15. Choose a unique name that would stand out from that of your competitors, and then, draw people to you.

16. Give your final name choice a think-through before proceeding to register it. Once it is registered, it could get nearly impossible to change the name. Also, marking shirts and other things with permanent logos with the name of your business on them can end up being a waste if you have to later on change it.

Cost of Running a Food Trucking Business

Another thing that needs your attention before you start a food truck business is the cost you could incur. First of all, you must note that the overall cost you spend on this business can be worth it as long as you make enough profit from it. And for that to happen, you must come up with some strategy that is different from the style others have followed. If you make the right business decisions, you could find yourself making more than five hundred thousand dollars per year.

The total cost that can be incurred in starting up a food truck business should be something in the range of forty thousand and two hundred thousand dollars. Most times, the price depends on where you are located, the cooking utensils you plan on utilizing, as well as the kind of truck you need to get for yourself. For example, you'd spend more purchasing a new truck than you would on a second-hand truck.

Now, we'd take a look at what you'd need to budget your money for.

Food Truck Startup Item	Cost of Item
One Time Cost	
Buying a Food Truck	$5,000 – $125,000
Inspection of the Truck	$100 – $500
Retrofitting and bringing your truck to code	$25,000 – $50,000
Generator	$1,500 – $10,000
POS software and hardware system	$500 – $1500
Paint	$1,000 – $3,000
Truck Wrap	$2,500 – $5,000
Initial Food Purchases	$500 – $2,000
Utensils, Papers, and Goods	$500 – $2,000
Website Design	$500 – $3,500
Initial Office Equipment and Supplies	$200 – $1,000
Advertising and Public Relations	$500 –$2,000
Consultation fees (Legal and Professional)	$500 – $2,000
Recurring Cost	
Payroll of about four staffers	$1,500 – $3,500
Commercial Kitchen rent	$500 —$3,000
Monthly Credit Card Processing Fees	3% of sales
Fuel	$250 — $400
Insurance	$5,000
Permits and Licensing	$50 – $10,000
Total Estimated Costs	**$40.000 – $200,000**

The total amount of money estimated from the items listed above can be pretty overwhelming for a few people, as they don't have the means to afford such an amount of capital. That is why you need to finance your business. You have to be sure that even when you loan the money that you'd be able to repay it without running out of business. Below are a few options through which you could get capital for your business though;

1. Equipment loan or financing projects: This is one where the sellers of a truck or those that finance equipment give you a loan that would help you in purchasing the rock.
2. Rollover for business startups: Once you have more than fifty thousand dollars in your retirement account, you could easily set up a rollover business startup account. The account allows you the grace of using the funds in your retirement account to begin your business without you paying the consequences for an early withdrawal.
3. Business credit cards: This option is good for you if you know you can handle debts pretty well.

4. Personal loan: This option is also good for those that have good credit scores and need an amount of money that is less than fifty thousand dollars.

5. Loans from small business administrations: The kind of loans you can get here are the small ones that will be just enough to cover most of the bills during the startup of your business.

6. You could find people to invest in your business: Family members, friends, and other interested folks could contribute greatly in ensuring that your concept is brought alive. To encourage investments, ensure that you have an attractive and convincing concept laid out.

7. Crowdfunding: This medium involves you reaching out to the public for funds. You could work via campaigns and all sorts of other ways you think would get them to contribute to your business.

8. Leasing: You could lease a used truck instead of going ahead to purchase one yourself. This leased truck usually would contain all the equipment you need. So, all you'd need is the leasing fee.

Ensure that you plan out how you want the money you get from any of these sources before you begin to spend them. Map out what would be incurred in buying trucks, purchasing cooking utensils, and all the other needed equipment. You must also ensure that you do not forget to include how you plan on paying back any borrowed funds. Usually, your gross revenue would cover all of those borrowed funds.

How to Finance Your Food Truck Business

The idea of finance is one thing that might hit a few people strongly, as indeed, financing a food truck isn't exactly easy. Food truck is less expensive than setting up an actual restaurant, but then, you'd still have to spend money on one or two things. That is why the idea of food truck financing is out there, to support those who desire to be owners of these businesses with loans and the necessary inventories.

Although we touched briefly on these finance options earlier, however, we would discuss in a little more detail a couple of options that you can work with to finance your food truck. The options usually vary in terms of the amount that is open for you to borrow, and the cost of the loan. So, at this point, you must take your time to check out two or more different options, to know which suits you best. This is the time you determine which option offers the best deals.

Examples of these options include;

1. Equipment financing
2. SBA Microloans
3. Business Lines of Credit
4. Business Credit Cards
5. Crowdfunding campaigns.

Equipment Financing

This kind of financing is best for you if you need the funds quickly, with very low interest attached to it. So, if you need funds to purchase a stove, grilling machine, oven, or some other cooking utensil, the best option comes out as equipment financing.

These loans work in such a way that the equipment you buy becomes the collateral for the loan. So, in case of a default, the equipment is taken away from you by the lender.

To finance your food truck, you could consider commercial vehicle loans. The reason you'd get low interest rates when you choose equipment financing is because of the kind of collateral that is required.

Lastly, you could also consider leasing out the equipment you need, as well as the vehicle. Here, you would just need to pay a couple of fees either monthly or yearly to use them. However, the only issue here is that the equipment will never really be yours at the end of the day.

SBA Microloans

This loan is great if you need to loan out a little amount of money. The SBA Microloan is a program that loans about $50,000 to business owners so that they can buy the supplies and equipment that they need for their businesses. These loans also could stand in as a starting capital for any business owner.

To apply for the SBA Microloan, all you have to do is go through the Microloan Intermediary. The minimum amount of money you can lend here is about $13000. Some banks would rather loan out higher amounts of money, so, if you are someone with needs that shoots to about $50,000, you could consider this.

Lastly, to pass for the acquirement of this loan, you would be required to present something as collateral.

Business Lines of Credit

This kind of financing is best when you need a starting capital that you can work with. This option differs from a loan in that it gives you a lump amount of money at once. Then, consequently, you make the payments. For a line of credit, when you take a particular amount of money, it has to be when you need it. Then, you pay that amount back.

For example, if you are cleared for a $100,000 line of credit, and you at that moment need about $5,000 to buy an oven. What the line of credit, you can borrow that particular amount of money you need, and then, pay it back. So, in a time range of say, six months, if you need another $17,000 for other things, your lender could help you merge the two draws on your credit into just a single monthly payment.

Here, you can borrow funds that fall in the range of $10000 and $1,000,000.

Business Credit Cards

This is the kind of financing you need when you need funds that you could easily pay off. This kind of financing could come out as expensive, but then, it could help in several scenarios.

If you need to get something very quickly, maybe in a state of emergency, and you at that moment do not have the cash to fund it, you could work with the business credit card financing. All you just need to note is that here, you'd need to pay very quickly to avoid the ugly effects of interest rates.

Several of these business credit cards provide about 0% APR, but then, several others still have arrangements that allow you the grace of earning points that can be activated for travel expenses.

Crowdfunding Campaigns

This kind of campaign is what you need for your brand when you want funding that is free from the effects of interest. To get started, all you need to do is activate websites like GoFundMe, and Kickstarter. This way, you get to raise enough money both from those that are pros at investing, and those that just desire to support what you do as a business.

There are different ways by which you can go about this funding method. Some of these websites would require that you pay back whatever money is invested in your business, while the others would require that you present your investors with something appreciative in form. You might also need to pay a couple of fees to whatever platforms you use for crowdfunding, as well as extra fees that would be charged by your PayPal account.

How to qualify for food truck financing?

There are different requirements that you might have to provide to be able to qualify for a food truck finance, and here, we would be looking at a couple of them. First of all, you need to know that some of these platforms require that you should have been coordinating your business for a time well over six months. Then, you should also have monthly revenue that runs into $10,000.

Some other times, you may be required to make collateral available as a down payment. That method is usually adopted when your credit isn't up to the minimum amount required. If you are thinking of securing a food truck equipment loan, you could be asked to pay a sum of money that falls in the range of 5-20% of the cost price. A couple of lenders might require that you have a proper UCC filing, and that works to effect how much you can qualify for some other kind of financing.

What kind of credit score do you need to have to buy a truck?

The credit score requirements usually differ from one lender to another, but then, you should be able to present something in the range of 550 and 640. The higher your credit score is, the lower the fees you would get when financing your food truck. Another thing that a high credit score would fetch you is a lesser initial payment that you have to settle before you are loaned the needed funds.

Knowing the possibility of your financing being stopped by bad credit

You need to first know that the several financing options that were listed above are weighed using different criteria. An example of the factors used for weighing is your business and personal credit scores. If you have a credit score that isn't all too high, you have to ensure that you find a platform that offers a moderate interest rate.

For commercial vehicle loans, you could work with low credit scores since what you'd be using as collateral is the equipment you buy. So, this method effectively prevents a situation where you have to pay off loans given to you by banks.

Another thing you might want to take note of is the fact that low credit can make the cost of a food truck loan spiral up. So, to qualify for more advantageous terms, you might want to spend a little time building your credit score to something quite acceptable.

Food Truck Financing Rates and Terms

The different rates and terms that a lender would make available to you depend largely on how much you qualify for and how your credit style looks like. It also depends on the kind of financing method that you choose to work with.

For equipment loans, you could borrow millions of dollars, and then, get a repayment term that runs within a bracket of one to six years. The yearly percentage rate usually would shoot off at three percent.

SBA microloans allow you to take loans as much as $50,000, with interest rates as low as 0%. The terms for the loans they offer you usually could run into six years or something in that range.

For crowdfunding, there's no limit on the amount of money you can get for your business. Although, you might have to pay a couple of funds to the platforms and websites on which you search for funds. The fee usually is about five percent of whatever you get. Then, you should also consider the charges tied to the transactions via PayPal or credit cards, which is about 3-5%. Here, to get the amount of money you need to fund your business, you should increase whatever target that the potential investors see.

Food truck lines of credit allow you to borrow as much as $250,000 with interest rates of about five percent.

As for credit cards, you should search for a zero percent APR. Using that technique will prevent your interest rates from soaring up to something in the range of 13 and 20%. If you also choose to only pay the minimum pay at the end of the month, the total cost that would be incurred in financing your business could eventually add up to a lot of money.

Deciding on The Location of Your Food Truck

Now is the time to make your decision on where you need your food truck to be parked? What are the factors you should first consider before choosing any site? Now, as a food truck business owner, the very first thing you want to pay attention to is the location of your food truck. It comes out as the most important factor, and here, we will look at the several methods you can employ in choosing locations where you can maximum profit.

Street Parking

Parking along the street could be one of the very sensible options you could vie for as a food truck business owner. But then, the issue lies in the fact that it isn't very easy to find streets that allow for that kind of trading. To solve the issue, you might want to first determine who your products are for—kids, adults, or the aged. The moment you get an answer to that, you have to pick out the one place you'd find several of your target customers in. For example, if your products are for kids, you might want to fix your truck in parks, or areas close to schools. Paying attention to these key things would no doubt fetch you the needed response in time.

Food Truck Parks

Food truck parks usually contain several food trucks selling in the same area. The first thing that could come to your mind is how bad this could be since there'd be a lot of competition, but then, there are several good sides to this. For example, a park with several food trucks would attract more attention than a single food truck would. Also, since there would be creativity employed by each of the truck owners, the customers would be able to make choices out of the many available. This idea could also be excellent if you set your food truck next to something that tops up your product. For example, if you, as a food truck business owner makes pizza, setting your truck next to some other truck that sells iced cream comes as the best option.

Business Districts and Large Office Buildings

This could come as a very excellent idea if the city in which these buildings are located allows for the operation of food trucks. All you just need to do is park the truck in a location where the workers could easily purchase your products during their breaks. Going for the downtown areas comes as one great option.

Successful food trucks usually fuse marketing skills into their businesses when they have to make location choices. All they need to do is get in touch with the administrators of the large office buildings who would allow them the chance of supplying food to the employees. To get them to know more about what you would be offering them as products, you could make extremely detailed flyers that would inform them of when you would be at the locations and the items you would make available to them.

Farmers Markets

Locating your food truck along the lanes that a farmer would market his goods can be a very good option as it offers you the chance to make use of fresh and quality ingredients in the production of your farm produce. All you need to do is to test the market, and then, see that it can fetch you as many customers as possible.

Bars and Clubs

The night is the very time people close off from work, and during that time, they get very hungry for delicious foods. You could target places that explode with a lot of entertainment or the other nightclub spots that are well known in the city.

To get a better response, you could also get in touch with the administration members of any bar around you, so that they can allow you the grace of using their property as a point for you to make money. So, if you are the kind of person that doesn't mind working late into the night, you might want to consider bars and clubs for your food truck business location.

Festivals, Events, and Sports Venues

Honestly, you would agree that a food truck business owner would inarguably make the best profits at sports venues and other centers where people gather massively. There, you'd find all sorts of customers who are more than willing to spend money just to have fun. If you cannot lay your hands on a space inside, you could be lucky to set up outside and trust me, with the right ideas, the people won't miss you.

Gas Stations

Finding a gas station where several people frequent during the day can be one way for you to make money through your food truck business. You could offer food items like burgers, sandwiches, and cold drinks that would help people relax under the hot sun. If you park at a gas station that is just near a highway or at the junction between states, the travelers could make a stop at your truck and then, buy whatever it is you are selling. But then, it is more than necessary that you make inquiries from the owner of the food truck station first before going ahead to sell within the coordinates.

College Campuses

This location comes as another very excellent option you could work with. Campus students remain one of the very people that purchase heavily when they see food trucks around. However, you might need to obtain permission from the authorities at the college before setting your food truck within the campus. It'd be a great idea to target the moments when they have football or basketball games.

Tips that would guide you in making maximum profits

1. The Staging Car: One of the things you can do to ensure that you make maximum profits is by considering the idea of a staging car that you'd send to wherever location you plan on working with. It is this stage car that would secure your land plot before another truck can lay claim on it.

2. Engage the media: Now that the world is hugely turning digital, you have to ensure that you make the best use of it. You want to see that you make your business the talk of the town on sites like Twitter and Facebook by letting the people know of the menus you make, and the several discount prices available. You would also want to ensure that you include your location so that your customers can know where you are.

Food Menu and Pricing

Food Menu

How can you craft up a food menu as a food trucking business owner? This question comes as one of the very essential things that you must ask yourself as you journey into this business. Your answer will drive several other things like the name of your truck, the kind of brand you want to ascribe to it, and the techniques you would go by when marketing. Here, a few tips about this topic will be discussed.

Food Menu Selection

The food item you want to offer

First, it is necessary to know the kind of food you want to offer to your customers. This is where you sit down and think of what food items you are good at making? What food will you make that will give maximum satisfaction to them? While doing that, you also want to consider the fact that you have other businesses out there acting as competition.

You should also take note of the fact that more menu items mean that you do more work. You also want to see that all the ingredients you need would not eat up too much of your truck's working space. If you are however going to make more than two dishes, ensure that you tag some as special dishes so that your customers know that their availability would be purely periodic.

Spice up your special cuisines with a unique touch

You could transform even the simplest dishes into something very amazing by adding your own ingredients. Usually, these ingredients are the things that draw the eye of your customers to your food. So, ensure that you add the necessary spices, and flavorings while ensuring that your food remains of top-notch quality. This technique doesn't mean that you change the ingredients you work with. Just see that you uniquely serve your food items.

Entertain spectacular product names

When selling your food items, you can make yours different from what everyone else uses. The difference usually is another thing that attracts maximum sales.

The drink menu

Getting a coffee brewing machine in your food truck is one nice concept you can work with. In fact, it comes out better when you supply it in the winter. So, while your customers get what they want, they also get something to warm up their insides.

Stocking Up on Ingredients

This section describes a process by which you gather the food items that you would be working with in your food truck. You want to see that you get exactly what you need to avoid wastage. When stocking up, you should also make it a habit to make your orders beforehand so that you aren't delayed along the line. It is also mandatory for you to know how to preserve the ingredients you buy, if perishable.

A few tips you could employ in this section include the following;

1. You can work with people that distribute food items in wholesale quantities: A few of some sites that you can find these people include Food Service.com. You could also check around your area for them.
2. You can visit the manufacturers yourself: This option really would save you the extra cost that the presence of middlemen can make you incur. You can find these people online, or visit smaller

companies that make your desired food items available. To ensure that you aren't spending way more than necessary, ensure that you juxtapose the prices given by the manufacturers.

3. You can search for suppliers in your local regions: Examples of these suppliers include the Cheney brothers in the Southeast.

4. You can visit farms and farmer's markets: This option is one that you should go for if you want very natural and quality ingredients. Here, you can also end up getting ingredients at a very cheap price. If the things you need to get from the farms aren't exactly pocket-friendly, all you need to do is increase the price of your food items a little more.

5. Food cooperative businesses: This option allows you to get all the food items you want to work with in large quantities. This way, you would be able to get a discount on everything that you buy. A food cooperative business is created when you and some other people who are interested in getting the same food items as you pair up and order for them collectively.

6. Shopping clubs: These clubs mostly would require you to present a membership fee that allows you to get as many food items as you want at very moderate prices. Examples of these clubs are the Restaurant Depot and Sam's Club.

How to properly stock up on ingredients

Now, you need to study how you can get a perfect storage option and other factors that will aid your stocking.

1. **Plan out how you want to store the food items:** One of the major issues that most food truck businesses face is how they can store the ingredients they purchase. So, you must consider the space of your food truck before getting your items. That way, you would be able to cancel out the unnecessary food supplies.

2. **Ensure that you have a record for your sales and inventories:** This idea helps you to ascertain the number of food items you need for a particular menu offer. Inventories will also help you to know the amount of whatever it is that you need.

3. **Picking out your suppliers:** There are several options you can go for when you get to this point.

There are wholesalers, retailers, and even stores where you can get your groceries. All you need to do is see which of them suit your taste best, and which would be friendly to your pocket.

4. **Receiving your order:** Since food trucks are so mobile that they don't have fixed addresses, you may find it hard to make orders. The best solution to this issue is to plan out a point of meeting with your suppliers. After getting the food items that you need, you should also ensure that you check to see that you got all you requested for.

5. **Dealing with waste and maximizing your profit:** Knowing how to properly store your ingredients is one way to solve this issue. You have to ensure that you don't buy a perishable food item if you won't be using it for another two weeks. This technique will go a long way to prevent you from having to lose money.

Food Pricing

This is the stage that falls under the startup phase of a food truck business plan. And, out of all the several things that any food truck owner has to go through, this comes out as one of the most demanding. Menu pricing is a task that you have to recurringly alter, to meet with the changes in the market and to also compete meaningfully.

Pricing Tips

So, now, we would look at the various things that you might want to pay attention to when setting a price for your menu items.

1. The cost of the food items: Now, you want to know how much exactly you are spending to get the ingredients for whatever you are supplying to your customers. You would find out that food items like lobster rolls tend to have prices that are way higher than the other simpler ones on the menu like French fries. So, the more money you spend getting the needed ingredients, the higher the cost at which the food item will be sold.

   Another thing that can hike the price is the quality of the ingredient you are using. Local and organic ingredients usually would require that you spend more money in the long run. So, ensure that you break down the cost of the ingredients that you use in preparing a dish so that it would serve as a platform for your menu pricing.

2. Miscellaneous expenses: Apart from the money you spend acquiring the food items needed, you also want to ensure that you add other expenses like the one you incur in acquiring labor, rent, and other unforeseen circumstances. If the dishes you make require that you spend a lot of money hiring professional staffers, then, you would need to consider that factor when determining the price of your menu.

3. Changes in the Market: This is a very important factor that you need to consider when determining your menu prices. Poor growing seasons can work to hugely affect the price of fruits and veggies. So, you might want to create space for some flexibility with your menu pricing so that you can respond well to the changes in the market. You might also want to ensure that you have good explanations to present to your customers when you have to adjust a particular menu price.

4. Customer Base: It is more than important to know the kind of people you are offering your services to. If you are offering to students, you have to be careful of how you increase your prices as they aren't really into any jobs yet. You also would want to take note of how the changes in your pricing system affect the way your customers respond to a change in price.

5. Competition: This factor can be seen in how much the food industry has grown today. You need to take note of the fact that customers can easily find some other place to get the same thing you are selling, and this gets worse in highly competitive areas. So, to fight this issue, you want to make sure that the prices of your menu items are not more than the prices of the menu of your competitors. This competition isn't just restricted to your area though. You might want to check out the restaurants around too to have a good idea. Now, this doesn't mean that you should choose prices that are in no way convenient for you. If you are going to go for high prices, ensure that

you deliver the best to your customers so that they can keep coming back for more.

6. Questions you need to ask yourself: Before you fix any price, there are several questions that you must first answer. Here, we will look at a few of them, to help you get the best prices.

   - What kind of menu item is your product? Is it something you'd have as a main course, dessert, or side meal?
   - How much labor would you need to get it done?
   - Does it require an ingredient that can only be found seasonally?
   - What are your competitors charging others for the same items?
   - What is the cost you desire to charge your customers?
   - How large should each serving be?
   - What time should your product be eaten? Morning, afternoon, or night?
   - Do you have side dishes to serve with it?
   - What is the perishability rate of your product?

Most of these questions would go a long way in helping you determine the price to sell your products at. So, you might need to ensure that you intuitively consider each one of them so that your customers can come back for more.

Methods of Pricing

The prices you set for your menu items generally affect what you can sell, and the cover costs. Now, you want to see how you can come up with the best prices, to make maximum profit. Here, we will discuss a couple of these methods.

1. Food-cost percentage pricing: This method of pricing is one that you want to adopt, as it is the most commonly used one. It involves you knowing the target food-cost percentage and the cost of the actual food for the item.

   The formula used for this pricing is; Food Cost ÷ Target Food-Cost Percentage = Menu Price

   For example, if you have an item like hamburger on your menu, with a food cost of about $1.50, and your target food-cost price is 35%, you make your calculations this way;

$1.50 ÷ 0.35 = $4.30

To have a rough idea of how the different cost percentages take a toll on the prices you set, you could take a look at the numbers below;

Percentage	Food Cost	Menu Price (min)
20	$1.50	$7.50
25	$1.50	$6.00
30	$1.50	$5.00
35	$1.50	$4.30
40	$1.50	$3.75

The issue with this method of pricing is in the fact that it does not consider factors like labor or other costs incurred in other operational processes.

2. Factor pricing: This method employs a factor such as 30% (i.e., the food cost percentage) in determining the price of your menu item. All you just have to do is multiply the food cost by your pricing factor.

To calculate the pricing factor and the menu price, all you need to do is gather the food-cost percentages and the actual food cost of the item. Then, you insert the figures into these formulae;

$100 \div$ Target Food-Cost Percentage $=$ Pricing Factor

Food Cost $\times$ Pricing Factor $=$ Pmenu Price

For example, if the target food-cost percentage is thirty percent, you divide 100 by 30 to get a value of 3.33. That is the pricing factor. If the food cost is \$1.50, you use the figure you got as the pricing factor to multiply it.

$\$1.50 \times 3.33 = \$5.00$

The issue with this kind of pricing method is the fact that it does not consider the fact that some foods have a higher cost than others. So, you might end up overpricing expensive food items and underpricing the cheap ones.

Chapter 3

Business Plan Development

As a new food truck business owner, you need to have an organized plan that would help you answer all your potential questions. And that is exactly what we would be doing here. What are the questions you need to ask yourself? And under what factors should you consider them? What are the strategies you need to learn to handle a business and how should you go about them? This phase is also very important because it could help you in obtaining a loan to finance your food truck business.

Executive Summary

This is the first thing that your business plan should contain. It has to be strong enough to leave a meaningful impression on the reader, in that it is short and meaningful. Here, you focus intently on who your company is, and how you expect it to grow into something big. You also will need to point out why your food truck business will be worth the shot.

You want to be sure you identify the role your business is playing in the market, and how it would fill in the gaps meaningfully. Ensure that you populate this section with very meaningful ideas, as well as details about your background, as this is the first part that any potential investor would first read.

Now, unto the key things you should focus on while writing the executive summary;

1. The kind of food you want to make available.
2. Where you want to sell your food.
3. Why your food choice will fetch maximum profit in the desired location.
4. The cost and profit you would get from your food truck business.
5. The future goals for your food truck business.

Company Description

This is the section that should be populated with details of your business plan. You want to describe how the business will be very beneficial to the existing market. What are the new things you are bringing to the table? What things are you changing? Give your potential investors a reason to consider you and what you offer.

Now, as regards the questions you should provide answers to, we will be discussing a couple here;

1. What kind of food truck do you plan on using? A truck, trailer, or food cart?
2. The reason for your choice is the question above.
3. Whether or not you plan on making your food in a truck or commissary kitchen.
4. How your product choice will compete with the menu items of the restaurants in your target location.
5. The specific consumer niche you plan on serving.
6. Your general competitive advantage.

Market Analysis

This is the section where you explain in detail how you plan on fitting your business into the market that already exists. You must do your research deeply before building on any of your points.

1. You would need to explain how the food industry is, the trends and growth patterns, the consumer gaps, and so on.
2. Identify the age groups, geographic area, and socioeconomic status of your target market.

3. Determine the size and growth potential of your target market.
4. Explain how you plan on gaining a large percentage of the market share in your location.
5. Expatiate on your pricing structure and other important financial information.
6. Mark out your competitors, and explain how you plan on contending with them.
7. Make mention of the food codes and other regulations that will affect your business.

Organization and Management

The next thing to do is to talk about how you plan on organizing and managing things. This section might not be necessary though if you plan on opening something that is just run by you and some other person. That is why you might need to mark out the responsibilities from the start to prevent confusion as your market develops. Talk about your management team, details on the ownership of the company, the salary and other benefits your workers would be opportune to receive, and the growth span they can work their way through. Below are a couple of details you might want to include in this section.

61

1. What kind of legal structure are you basing your business upon? Sole proprietorship or partnership?
2. What are the full names of your owners?
3. What is the percentage that is liable to each of the owners?
4. What is the type of ownership here?
5. Details as regards the stocks.
6. The full name of those on your management team.
7. The primary responsibilities of those on the team.
8. The educational background of those on your team.
9. The previous employment of those on your team.
10. The necessary experience and skills would help your business to be successful.
11. Recognition of the food industry.
12. Salary paid to those in the management team.

Service or Product Line

This is the section where you use the talk extensively on the items made available on your food truck. What are the things that are unique to your product? What things do you plan on using to draw people to you? Talk about your ideas, and explain how you plan on keeping the demand for your products high. Here are a few other things you might want to include;

1. What type of cuisine do you plan on offering?
2. Why you chose that particular cuisine.
3. Why customers would want to eat your food.
4. What is the competitive advantage?
5. Are your recipes properly founded or still in development?
6. How do you plan on launching new menu items?
7. Do you already have customers who know you in the target market?
8. What do you think could cause your customers to demand your products less.
9. Will you need your staff to sign non-compete agreements?
10. How do you plan on making changes to your menu with time?
11. Would you or would you not be developing new products.
12. Do you or do you not plan on owning several food trucks later on.

13. How do you plan on extending your services—event bookings, etc.

Marketing and Sales

This section is where you talk about how you plan on being loyal to your customers. You will need to talk about the various strategies you have planned out to keep them happy and satisfied. It's also important that you target the quality and originality of whatever it is you are making available.

1. Do you plan on setting prices that are lower than the ones set by your competitors?
2. Do you plan on offering products that no one has seen before?
3. Do you plan on increasing your staff as time goes on?
4. Do you plan on buying more food trucks?
5. Do you plan on extending your services to geographical areas?
6. Do you plan to sell from your truck only?
7. Do you plan on attending food truck fairs?
8. How do you plan on reaching out to your customers?

9. How do you plan on making your business known on social media?
10. Do you have special offers for customers when they return?
11. Do you have incidences of free samples?
12. How do you plan on creating an interactive map for customers to locate your truck?
13. How many days do you plan on taking off in a year?
14. Do you plan on selling throughout the winter or are your sales just restricted to the warm months?

Funding Request

Not all the business plans have this section included, but it will help you to know how much a food truck costs, and how you would get the funds for it. `You would also be opportune to know how much you would need for the general funding, insurance, and other necessary licenses. Here are some very important questions you might want to answer;

1. How much capital do you need to start?
2. Do you think you would need more funding later in the future?

3. How do you plan on using the funds you are awarded?
4. How do you plan on paying back your loans?
5. What does a potential investor get in a case where your food truck does well?
6. How do you think these funds would create opportunities for your truck?

Financial Projections

Lastly, it is important to set out your financial goals. If you have been in this business before, you might want to include the financial data you accumulated in the past. However, as a beginner, you will need to estimate how you can make money over a particular time frame using realistic assumptions. Ensure that these estimates resonate well with your funding request though.

Chapter 4

The Rules and Regulations

This section is where we pay more attention to the various legal requirements that you would need to take note of before you begin your food truck business. Most of the rules binding the business differ from one city to the other, and so, to avoid getting into legal problems, you should study this section carefully. Here, we would look at a few of these rules that guide a food truck business.

Establish The Structure of Your Business

Now, before you go ahead to set up the structure of your food truck business, you have to first determine whether you would be operating as a sole proprietor, or with the help of some other partners. The latter is known as a partnership business. Now, you could also choose to make your business a corporation, and indeed, that will go a long way in ensuring that your assets are protected from any loss the business suffers. This is what is referred to as a limited liability business.

Limited liability, just like the name implies helps to streamline the losses your business suffers to itself. So, it's almost like your business is an entity on its own that is responsible for its risks and losses. So, if it is issued or in debt, your assets would not be affected. To get your business incorporated, you should commune with a lawyer who would guide you on the right paths to follow.

Incorporating a business brings along with it extra costs and requirements, and a few of them include;

1. Filing fees
2. Publication fees
3. Franchise taxes
4. Legal fees
5. Corporate recordkeeping, etc.

Now, the things listed above could lead to you spending more time setting up your company than normal, and so, it is advisable to wait until a later date before getting it incorporated. If you plan on setting up a sole proprietorship kind of business, you could just get your business registered. Then, you proceed to get a doing business certificate which can be acquired at a small cost. The rest procedures can then be finished online.

Obtain Your EIN

EIN is an acronym that stands for Employer Identification Number. In a food truck business, it cannot be an easy task to manage your business, organize the kitchen, and then, attend to the customers by yourself, all at the same time. This issue is why you need to employ people who would work under you to make things a lot easier.

For that very reason, you need to get an EIN for every one of your employees from the IRS. Then, get an I-9 form for each one of them, and then, have them fill out a W-4 form. You will also need to attend to your payroll tax duties, which include you paying the employer's share of social security and Medicare taxes. You will also need to deduct a particular fraction of the earnings of your employees to settle the state and federal income taxes. Lastly, you will also need to pay your worker's compensation insurance.

Get The Necessary Permits and Licenses

Getting the needed permits and licenses is crucial when planning out a food truck business. Failure to attend to this aspect usually is a recipe for instant trouble with the law. You might also have to spend all your profits on fines or end up closing your business forcefully.

Here, we will take a look at some of the licenses that are very important for you to get for your business.

Food Service Business License

Before you can run a food truck business, you must first ensure that you have this license. You will readily get this license from the city that you plan on running your business in. Some cities require that you renew your businesses once every year. Sometimes, it may be once in two years. So, to prevent your license from expiring, you must ensure that you renew it constantly.

When acquiring a food service business license, you must state the purpose of your business' existence. For services that are strictly related to food services, your purpose could be the supply of services like gluten-free meal delivery. So, to ensure that your license is approved, ensure that you are as specific as possible.

Food Handler's License

This license is issued by the city where you want your food truck to be located. It validates you serving food to the residents. The requirements for this license differ from place to place, and sometimes, you might need to be examined before you obtain it. To avoid failing this test, there are several training courses you can take that can effectively prepare you.

Health and Safety Permit

One thing that you should know as a food truck business owner is that it is not enough to just get all the required licenses. You would still need to renew them as at when due. The reason for this continual renewal is because health officials usually would map out frequent checks on the truck, to ensure that it meets all the food safety requirements. And that is another thing you need to be careful of, as you can have your business shut down if the requirements are not met.

A few things that the health inspectors check for in food truck vehicles include;

1. The storage of food. You want to ensure that the food is stored under hygienic conditions, and at the right temperature.
2. Whether or not the people handling the food are wearing gloves or not.
3. Whether or not the equipment used for cooking is clean or not.
4. Whether or not your food truck meets all the health and fire codes.

Gas and Electricity Permit

Food trucks are essential for cooking, and cooking deals with fire. And to get fire running, you'd need either gas or electricity. Now, the kind of equipment you use for cooking has to be the kind that is free from all hazards and risks. To ensure that you are on the safe side always, ensure that you run periodic checks on the equipment to see if there's anything that needs to be changed or repaired. You do not want a situation where some authority comes around and finds fault in any of your equipment.

Commercial Vehicle License

The food truck you use for your business is another of the many things you need to get a license for. The licenses that are awarded to vehicles usually depend on their weights, lengths, and heights.

Driver's License

First, you need to ascertain who would be driving your food truck. If you will be hiring someone, you must ensure that he or she has a driver's license. The same goes for you if you would be driving the truck yourself. Driver's license is a very important requirement that allows you to drive a food truck on public roads. You also should check out the dates your license expires so that you can get it renewed as soon as possible.

Insure Your Food Truck

Several states out there now require that your food truck business is protected by insurance. So, if you are using a truck, you might have to get your hands on commercial car insurance. If you plan on taking your vehicle to areas with a crowd, you would need general liability insurance. When you employ people to work for you, you would be required to pay a worker's insurance.

There are several categories of insurance that you might need to first settle, and they all depend on the kind of services you offer, as well as the nature of your business. Now, we would take a brief look at the different types of insurance that you could cover for your truck, so that you can know which one to work with.

1. Commercial Vehicle Insurance: This type of insurance helps to cover damages from accidents related to vehicles.

2. Property insurance: This insurance covers your truck and cooking equipment in case they are stolen.
3. General liability: This insurance helps to cover the damages that are not related to your vehicle.
4. Workers' comp: This insurance is worked within most states to fill in for the funds that employees spend due to accidents they sustain at work.
5. General auto insurance: This type of insurance varies from state to state, but then, runs to a figure of about $2400 a year.

It is also crucial that you know the factors that can affect the amount of money you spend insuring.

- Your coverage limits
- The kind of food truck you are using for business
- The state and city your food truck is sited in
- The value of the personal property you insured
- The different locations and events you attend each year
- Your time range of operation
- Seasonality of your food truck business

- How much equipment you have installed permanently and those that you can move around.

Zoning and Parking Restrictions

Many cities and towns today have several zone restrictions that prevent you from just parking your truck anywhere. Some of these restrictions work to reduce the movement of food trucks, and trailers to certain locations. To know these places, you could meet up with the county clerk. You may also be required to comply with the two-hour parking restrictions.

Ensure that while parking your truck, that you move near to the curb. See to it that you also do not double park. Ensure that you reach out to your local vehicle department to get more information though.

Chapter 5

Getting Your Food Truck

Now that we have laid out a lot of the important bits, it is time for you to decide on what food truck to get. What kind do you think would suit your business and why?

Available Options For a Food Truck

There are several choices of food trucks from which you can choose, and to know what suits you best, you should go through the ones listed below;

1. Food Trucks: This option allows for a lot of space and flexibility. So, you can both cook and serve within your food truck. The average size of a food truck ranges between 14 and 34 feet in length. However, sometimes, depending on the length of your truck and the features available in your truck, you might need to prepare your food in some other place—maybe at home.

2. Food Trailer: This vehicle option combines the features of a food truck and a food cart. The similarity it shares with a food cart is the fact that

they have to be towed to wherever they are to finally be set. The similarity it shares with a food truck on the other hand is the large room available in it. So, you get plenty of room for storage and cooking.

3. Food Carts: This vehicle option needs only little maintenance. They have simple structures and can easily be fixed to your cars before they are eventually pushed to the final destinations. However, before you choose a food cart, you have to be sure that you can work in a small space. You also might not be able to serve varieties of food in a food cart.

Do This Before Selecting a Truck

Before you chose any truck for your business, it is important to consider a few factors first.

1. What food item do you plan on serving?

   As a food truck business owner, you have to know what it is you plan on making available to your customers. To make the whole process worth it, ensure that you take note of all the stress that you would go through as you cook. The stress usually would play out in the number of processes you have to work with—from grinding to chopping, and so on. Then, you can go ahead to itemize all the tools you would need for these processes.

Lastly, you would have to take note of the exact place you need to store your equipment and tools when you cook and after.

2. Do you plan on cooking on-site or at home?
   The processes tied to this question all depend on whatever food item it is you have on your menu. Depending on the complexity tied to it, you could either cook on-site, that is, in your truck or at home. Some cities have some laws that forbid food truck business owners from cooking and storing food in their trucks, so, you have to be careful to know what rules have been set in yours. Now, if that is the case, you could do all your cooking in some commercial kitchen. At least, that would help ensure that your truck has more space for you to work with.

Preparing the food at home is also another very nice option. You wouldn't have to spend so much money and time going to commercial kitchens to make your meals.

3. What is the cost of the truck?

Before you choose what vehicle you want—food truck, food cart, or trailer, ensure that you have the capital that you need to buy a vehicle that won't pose a lot of problems in the nearest future. The growth of your business could also depend on your vehicle. Its structure and design are two things that can determine how customers flood in to buy from you.

You also need to be ready to attend to issues related to your vehicle's maintenance. Issues with your vehicle could cause you to go out of business for a whole day, so, you have got to be careful.

If you cannot afford to get a new truck, see that you get one that is at least, fairly used. That would go a long way in ensuring that you do not spend too much money on maintenance. If none of the options above seem good to you, do not hesitate to lease a truck.

4. Where do you plan on fixing your food truck?

As a food truck business owner, choosing the right location should be your goal. You are making food items for your customers, and you need to get those customers. So, when making your choices, ensure that you target areas that are populated by your target customers. Doing that would fetch you as much profit as possible.

Also, while considering the point above, you shouldn't forget to put the size of your cart into consideration. Food carts are small, and so, you most definitely would not need a lot of space to get them ready. Larger vehicles like your food truck would need that you get a larger parking space where you can sell your food items.

Lastly, ensure that you confirm what your city's laws on food truck parking correlate with what you have planned out. Most cities wouldn't want their sidewalks to be sites for your business, so, you have to be careful in general.

5. Considering your customers

You must take into consideration those to who you plan on delivering your food items. You should make this priority, even before you buy your truck. What menu do you think would appeal the most to them? Why is that what you think they want? How easy would it be to get them to buy from you?

Those questions would only help you to know the strategies you need to implement—the style of your truck, the offers you make available, and so on.

6. The number of people you plan to serve daily

As you begin your food truck business, you would notice that you get to sell to several people in a day. And really, it all gets better when you make quality food that gets people coming back for more. So, you need to plan out the number of people you can sell to in a day.

Doing that would guide you on the number of ingredients to buy, and the kind of equipment you would be needing to cook. If you have high demand, you might want to get a very large truck that allows you a lot of storage space for food and extra ingredients. This way, you would be able to quickly whip up something in case what is on the ground is exhausted.

7. The number of people that would be working for you.
   The answer you give to this question again depends on the kind of food it is you are serving. How complex is it to make it? Do you think you would need several people to help you get things done? Is it something you can handle by yourself? Do you think you'd need a cashier?

As you answer those questions, ensure that you also consider the space available for you to work in. You wouldn't want your employees to be crowded too much in a place. So, it is very important to see the layout you have, and then, see how you can organize your staff into their various duties.

Lastly, if you choose to get a food truck, take note of the fact that there has to be the right number of seatbelts for those who would be riding the truck. If there are not enough, you could just fix one or two in place, or prepare some other means of transport for your employees.

A Short message from the Author:

Hey, I hope you are enjoying the book? I would love to hear your thoughts!

Many readers do not know how hard reviews are to come by and how much they help an author.

I would be incredibly grateful if you could take just 60 seconds to write a short review on Amazon, even if it is a few sentences!

>> Click here to leave a quick review

Thanks for the time taken to share your thoughts!

Chapter 6

Designing Your Food Truck

Designing your food truck is one of the very last things you need to pay attention to. The outlook of your truck is what attracts people to you, and so, you want to ensure that you settle for something amazing. Now, while having it designed, you want to ensure that you are managing your working space. Know what you have on your menu, the equipment you need for that, and what your budget looks like. Once you do all of that, you are one step prepared. Now, we will be looking at this topic under a few other subheadings that would make your planning easier.

Selecting The Right Vehicle

Now, you could decide to buy your truck before thinking about the design you want to implement. And to be on the safer side, you could also choose to plan out your design before buying your truck. Both options depend on you and how meticulous you want to be. The latter comes out as the better idea though, as you would be able to see ahead what your food truck would look like. So, when you eventually get your truck, it would be something you choose based on the space you need for your equipment and staff.

When choosing the truck that you want to work with, you have to ensure that you consider a couple of options;

1. The size: The bigger the size of your truck, the more space you can allow for storage, cooking, and several other activities. It also determines how easy it would be to get a parking site.
2. The look: Ensure that whatever you are selling is what your truck looks like. This area is where you deal with aesthetics and a couple of other embellishments.
3. New vs. retrofitted: You could plan on either designing your truck right from the scratch, i.e., buying a new one with no designs on it at all. You could also choose to adopt one that has already been designed to your style.
4. Fuel: If you are going to cover a long distance before you get to your destination, you might want to consider how much fuel your vehicle consumes. Electric cars would save you the cost

of buying fuel, while fuel-driven cars can be used in areas that are proximal to you.

Once you can make your choices as regards the factors above, you can then move on to getting your equipment ready. The benefit of getting your truck's layout planned before you buy it will help you have an idea of the measurements you'd be working with.

Running Your Food Truck

Getting to run your food truck can be quite time-consuming and exhaustive, so, you need to settle down and plan out what you want. Doing this will help your business stay afloat with good profit recorded. To start with, here are a couple of questions you need to ask yourself;

1. How much voltage will my equipment be needing?
2. What are the rules guiding emissions in my target area?
3. How will my power supply affect my insurance rates?

Depending on what answers you give, there are several choices for you to work with.

- Generators: They come in different forms and sizes, and can run several equipments. The bigger it is, the more appliances it can power effectively. So, if you have refrigerators, drink fountains, ovens, lights, etc., you can be sure that you'd have no problem at all. Another very crucial thing to note is the fact that generators release a lot of heat and carbon monoxide, which is very poisonous to the blood. So, if you are going to use a generator, it has to be located at a place where you can breathe in air that is not its exhaust. You should also keep it from anything that tends to catch fire.

- Solar panels: Working with solar panels will go a long way in helping you run your truck and save money. They might be pretty expensive to get at first, but then, as you journey in your business journey, you discover how much of a nice investment they are. You could place them on your roof, but then, if you plan on storing things there, you might have to look for some other place where you can have them accessing the sunlight richly. The panels are flat enough to not take much space though. And yes, lastly, getting a solar panel will give you an edge when you market your truck.

- Fuel-powered generators: These generators are pretty much costly to run, and can release a lot of emissions too. Biodiesel engines, for example, run on vegetable oil, so, if you have appliances that consume a lot of power, you might end up incurring too much money on fuel.

Food Truck Layout

This is the stage where you have to increase your planning efforts. Note that whatever interior design you work with will affect your staff and customer directly. Also, the kitchen should be your priority. If it is not designed well enough, you might end up making your staff feel uncomfortable while they work. And that shouldn't be. A well-designed space promotes your staff's safety, happiness, and effectiveness. Here, we will take a look at a couple of things to take note of while planning the layout;

1. Durable, non-slip and inflammable floors that are made of vinyl or some other quality material.
2. Proper ventilation can be made possible with a hooded fan, vent in the roof, or several windows.

3. Room for movement of everyone working on the truck—note that several hot things would be moved about.
4. Easy access to inventories
5. Ease of movement between workstations.
6. Emergency exits.

It is very important to visualize how you want the food items to move—right from when they are delivered to the truck to the point that they get to the customer. Once you can study how the workflow will be, you'd be able to plan out your layout even better. A guide to achieving the best result can be seen below;

1. Plan out a space for refrigeration and storage
2. There should be an area where you prepare the food.
3. There should be a spot in the truck for grills, deep fryers, ovens, and stovetops.
4. Plating areas are essential.
5. Serving areas too should be your priority.
6. Clean-up stations.
7. Considering a hand-washing section will also be nice.

You could decide to design your food truck by yourself, but then, if you have the means to, you could also employ people to do it for you. Below are a couple of designers you can work with;

- In New York, you could try out the Shanghai Mobile Kitchen Solutions. They provide cooking equipment for Chinese kitchens.
- In Chicago, the Mr. Kustom company specializes in the building of food trucks. They know all the regulations in Chicago and will build your truck for you with them in mind. They can also help you with issues related to light, the internet, and vinyl wrapping.
- In Austin, the ATX Food Truck Builder is a family-owned company that offers print and design services. They are also the ones you should call for your electricity, and plumbing issues.
- Toronto's Unique Food Truck is the one company you need to employ to build and design your truck.
- The Apex Specialty Vehicles design food trucks anywhere across U.S and Canada.

One last thing that you need to consider when designing your truck's layout is whether you want a service window or an ambiance.

- A service window allows for only one way by which you can access your customers. The amount of space you require usually would depend on the food item you are serving.
- An ambiance will go a long way to protect your customers from the outer elements.

Food Truck Mobility

Even though you'd expect that a food truck moves about from one location to the other, you'd still find several that stay in a single place throughout the year. And really, it is up to you to decide whether you want to stay put in someplace or move around. But then, to aid your decision-making, we would look at each of the options to know their pros and cons.

- Staying in one place: This will allow you options like outdoor seats, reusable plates and other heavy dishware and public restrooms. And really, it's almost like those restaurant buildings have there that have to rely on the customers to find them. Deciding to stay in one place will

91

affect your design in several ways, and they include;

1. A smaller service window: You wouldn't have to go for a truck model with a large service window, since you only need something through which you can get their orders. After, you could have their food taken out to them. This style allows you to have more space for cooking and food preparation.

2. Interior decoration: You could choose to go for menu boards and some other sophisticated things since you would basically be using them in one place.

3. Reduced storage space for dishware: Reusable dishware would need little storage space, as compared to disposable ones. And the reason for that is because you could just clean them up as they are used. To ensure that this plan works out, ensure that you have someone cleaning consistently so that you do not run out of plates as you serve.

- Hitting the road: Really, the major issue that most restaurants face today is them getting the right set of customers. However, the moment you decide to go mobile, you can find customers for yourself and make more profit than you would do just by staying in one place. Now, as to how your movement will affect your design choices, here are a few considerations;

1. Storage space: When you move about from one place to the other, you would definitely not be able to have a seating area. So, most people would just have their food and then, leave. So, you would need to plan out space for dishware, cutlery, and other necessary equipment.

2. Equipment load: The amount of equipment you stack in your truck will hugely affect the efficiency of the fuel in your truck. It could also cause some serious wear and tear problems on your tires and brakes. So, it would probably be a good idea to travel light.

3. Material tear down: If you are going to set up some structure outside your truck—a sandwich board or garbage can, you have to ensure that it is something that you can easily set up and bring down. Then, it also has to have an area where you can store it.

4. Emergency equipment: The more you drive, the higher the risk of breathing down. So, you have to ensure that you get emergency car maintenance—a jack, a spare tire, fuses, and a basic toolkit.

Food Truck Branding

Now, we have come to the point where we emphasize the need to market your food truck. The difference between a food truck and an actual restaurant lies in the fact that the latter option involves you waiting for your customers to drive to you, while the former requires that you drive to them. So, to make things easier for you, you should consider making an exterior that would keep people attracted to your truck. Now, we would take a look at the options you should consider when branding the exterior of your truck;

- Vinyl wraps: They are the commonest ways to design your food truck, but then, they can be quite hard and costly to install. If it's something you can do yourself though, you should go ahead and do just that. However, if it is something that you need help with, do not hesitate to reach out to people who can help you with it. With a vinyl wrap, you could paste your logo and any other graphic design to your truck.

- Hand painting: One other option you could go for asides from using vinyl wraps is an actual painting done on the truck. This option is actually way cheaper and DIY-friendly. The only issue is that the logo you paint on your truck may not look exactly like whatever you have on your website. If you need your painting to stand out though, you might want to consider employing a graphics designer for the job.

Food Truck Bathrooms

The kind of bathroom you decide to use for your food truck business depends on several factors which include;

1. The rules and regulations in your area
2. The size of your truck
3. Your target location
4. Your personal choices.

The restroom rules differ generally from city to city. Some cities will require that you station your truck in an area with a washroom that has water running. For some other cities, you must not leave your truck unattended for long.

If you have the space for a restroom on your truck, it could come as being very productive as your workers don't have to go out of the truck. The only issue here is that you end up spending more money cleaning and maintaining your truck.

Chapter 7

Food Truck Supplies and Equipment

After getting your truck ready, the next thing you want to do is decide on the kind of equipment you want to have inside it. Having quality equipment in your food truck will go a long way to affect your sales, and then, help you maximize your profit. And because deciding on what you need in your truck can be very hard, we will be looking at a couple of these equipment to know what it is you need and what you don't. We will also study how you can make good use of whatever space you have in your food truck or cart.

1. Cooking equipment: The equipment you would be needing for cooking usually would be the one thing that would eat up a majority of the space in your truck. So, you have to ensure that you plan things the right way. First, there's the idea of using both countertops and actual models of your kitchen equipment. To generate more space for your work in the kitchen, you could allot spaces to the ones you use the most, and then, stick to the countertop for the equipment you wouldn't

be needing often. Here, we will see a few of the essential equipment you should get for your kitchen.

- A griddle or flat-top grill: This equipment is what you need to cook food items like pancakes, eggs and burgers.
- Range: This equipment allows you to pan fry, boil, and simmer anything.
- Charbroiler: It helps you to get the required grill marks, i.e., flavor on your chicken and steaks.
- Microwave: You can use this to heat or steam your vegetables.
- Toaster: It blesses your bread, sandwiches, waffles, and muffins with the right texture.
- Salamander: It helps you to keep the surface of your foods brown. Examples of these foods include macaroni and cheese.
- Fryer: This equipment allows you to cook several food items like fries, chicken tenders, and onion rings.
- Food truck exhaust hood: This hood is important to help you get rid of the dangerous grease vapors that your equipment produces.

2. Warming and Holding equipment: This equipment will help keep your food at safe temperatures. They also help to prevent foodborne illnesses and health inspection violations. So, generally, your food items remain appetizing to your customers. The equipment you should get to warm your food include the following;

- A countertop food warmer: This will help to keep foods like pasta, vegetables, and casseroles.
- Fry Dump Station: This will help to keep your fires warm
- Soup Warmer or Kettle: This will help to ensure that your soup is hot enough till you are ready to have it served.

3. Food preparation equipment: This equipment helps in your food preparation process.

- Stainless steel work blade: This tool helps to add to your workspace.
- Cutting boards: These boards serve as the perfect platforms when you need to slice, cut, and dice anything.
- Knives and Knife rack: Get good knives so that you don't have to keep spending money

replacing them. And when you get them, keep them in a knife rack to prevent injuries and accidents.

- Skillets: Skillets are also known as frying pans. Use them to pan fry, or steam your menu items.
- Saucepans: These pans help you to reduce, simmer, and steam your sauces and broths.
- Turners: You can use turners to cook anything and everything from burgers to veggies.
- Thermometers: You can use thermometers to ensure that your food items are cooked to the right temperature.
- Blender or Food Processor: A blender will be useful when making smoothies, salsa, and sauces.
- French fry cutter: This equipment will help you cut out a lot of time if you have fries on your menu.
4. Food Truck Supplies: Since you would be serving customers who are always on the go, you might need to get a whole lot of serving disposables. Ensure that you have enough room to store these supplies because you definitely do not want to run out of them. A few of them include the following;

- Serving utensils like spoons, ladles, or tongs.
- Pump Condition Dispenser
- Squeeze bottles
- Sugar, Spice, and cheese shakers
- Paper food trays
- Paper, foam, and plastic dinnerware
- Paper or plastic cups.
- Plastic utensils
- Take-out containers
- Portion cups
- Paper napkins
- Order forms
- Disposable gloves
- Aluminum of plastic food wrap.

5. Refrigeration equipment: This equipment will come in handy when you have to store your drinks, beverages, and sauces. Now, there are different types of equipment you will most likely need for this, and they include;

- Worktop refrigerator: This will go a long way to increase your working surface
- Sandwich or salad preparation refrigerator: This has a chilled cabinet, a top with space for your covered pans, and a strip of sauce for assembly.

- Pizza preparation refrigerator: They allow more workspace where you can assemble your pizzas.
- Countertop glass door refrigerator: This allows you to display your bottled beverages and drinks.
- Undercounter freezers: This is the perfect freezer for a food truck that allows you to store items like ice cream without you having to worry about space.
6. Janitorial equipment: These are the things that you need to maintain a clean environment.
- A three-compartment sink that allows you to wash, rinse and sanitize your dishware.
- A hand sink that allows you to wash your hands to maintain good hygiene.
- An anti-fatigue mat: This mat will prevent the area you stand on all the time from becoming prone to slipping.
- Sanitizing chemicals: These are chemicals for your dishware and other surfaces.
- Scrubs and sponges: These things help to keep the dishes and cooking utensils clean.
- Trash can and liners: These things help you to keep your waste disposal area clean.
- Broom and Dustpan.

Chapter 8

Procedures For Food Safety

There are several things that you need to consider when trying to keep your food safe. Several of the issues that are related to the management of a food truck usually are blamed on the owner, and the others on the size of the truck. When a food truck is small in size, it means that the food truck chefs would have a smaller space to work in. And that can lead to a lot of sanitary issues.

In other cases where trucks keep their ingredients on top of cabinets, they could also risk a situation where they get infected by rodents and other outer pests. Apart from the risk of contamination from the pests and other external factors, a few other risks include;

- Cross-contamination of the ready-to-eat-foods
- Inadequately sanitized surfaces
- Improper refrigeration
- Improper handwashing techniques.

All of these things end up posing a serious challenge to the food truck owners as you cannot be too sure of the safety of their foods. However, once you erect a couple of safety procedures, you would be good to go.

1. Wash your hands and ensure that you change your gloves regularly as you work. This safety tip might seem pretty obvious, but then, it is one way by which you can prevent foodborne illnesses. By ensuring that you wash your hands immediately and after you handle any kind of food will go a long way to ensure that you keep all things hygienic and safe. You also should ensure that your workers wash their hands after they touch money to protect the food items that your customers eat.

2. Ensure that you adequately store your refrigerated foods. To prevent the growth of microbes like bacteria or fungi, ensure that you store your foods at temperatures lower than 40-degree Fahrenheit. For this tip to be work though, you would need to have the right set of equipment on your truck to protect your food. You also should pay attention to the expiry dates on the packaged food items as after those dates, refrigeration would do nothing to help.

3. Clean and sanitize all the stations used for food preparation and cooking to prevent cross-contamination. Ensure that you clean all your utensils, cutting boards, pots, hands, and every other surface that gets in contact with food.

4. Familiarize yourself with all the local health codes by visiting your local and state health departments. Once you can manage your business within the standards set by health officials, you would hardly have any issues. To have an idea of the rules set by each state, you can browse through the FDA's website.

5. Keep a perfectly working thermometer in your truck. Regulating the temperature within your truck is one of the many challenges that most food businesses deal with. So, you have to see to it that you have a reliable temperature gauge that will help you to keep the temperatures in check while you serve food. That will inevitably prevent the spread of microorganisms.

6. Wash your products as often as possible without skipping any. Over time, several cases of food poisoning have been recorded, and most of them are related to bacterial infections. So, this issue

calls for the frequent rinsing of your ingredients and other products that would go into your cooking. This way, you would be able to get rid of pathogenic organisms and toxic bacteria.

Chapter 9

Hiring and Managing Your Team

Now that you have planned out the other things, it is time to now think of how you want to erect a workforce inside your truck. What kind of people do you need? What level of expertise do you need from them? How many of them can you employ? And how much are you willing to spend employing them? Let's delve into answering these questions.

First of all, if you are going to hire anyone to work with you, you should do it about two or three weeks before you begin this business. This time frame is important so that you can get them acquainted with what is necessary for them to know, and to ensure that they are familiar with the steps and procedures. You also want to see that the staff members you are recruiting are those that would be around for a long time. Having to frequently change your staff can be very demanding and bad for your business.

Now, we will discuss a few tips that would help you scale through the hurdle of hiring and managing your team.

1. Hire a food truck manager first: Your manager would be responsible for the following operations;
   - Training and managing the other staff members
   - Seeing to it that the rest of the staff follow the sanitary procedures and regulations
   - Following the health and safety guidelines
   - Managing the cash
   - Driving the truck

These activities, even though may appear simple, need to be handled by someone that is capable. He or she must enjoy working in a place where no idleness is allowed. Actually, it is the manager that sees to it that the right speed is maintained in the truck. And when any challenging situation occurs, your food truck manager has to be positive enough to stir up the staff members to keep going.

Lastly, you might also want to check through the person's record as a driver to see if he can handle the movement of a truck. You also want to know if he can boast of a clean driving record.

2. How many employees do you think you would need? The answer to this question lies in the size of your truck. The bigger your truck is, the more people it would be able to accommodate. Usually, the number that most food truck owners work with falls in the range of two to six. The other people you might need to employ in your truck apart from the manager include the chef, the cooks, the attendants that are to stay by the service window, and a couple of other people to make one or two preparations in the kitchen.

3. Write out your job description: Apart from details like the wages you would be paying your staff and the summary of what you need them to do, there are a few other key things you should not miss in this stage;
   - The location of the truck—is it stationary, or would you need your workers to travel?
   - Incidences of heavy object lifting.
   - The nature of the space they'd be working in—size, and temperature.
   - The working hours—evenings or weekends.
   - The requirements for a driver's license.

You might also want to let them know of the benefits they stand to get by working with you;

- Training sessions
- Flexible scheduling
- Free meals
- Healthcare

4. Make your job openings known to the public: The best platform to get this done is the use of online platforms. You could also advertise to students during their holidays to see if they'd be willing to work. To speed up this process, ensure that it is easy for job seekers to apply for jobs online. You could craft up application systems that would help you sort out those that you get. That technique will also help you to quickly figure out those with the talents you need.

5. Arrange interviews: Once you choose a particular set of people for work, you need to move on to the next stage which has to do with interviewing them. You could hold physical interview sessions or video sessions, all depending on what is convenient for you. One more thing that you can

do is to offer your applicants free food from the truck. The kind of questions you ask during your interview should help you to know how well they can work under pressure.

6. Employ workers: After the interviews, you definitely would find some category of people with the right set of skills and attributes you want to keep for yourself. For these sets, onboarding paperwork should be completed by the hired staff, and then, complete other checks—licenses, and background—before proceeding to train them for work.

Chapter 10

Advertising Your Food Truck Business

Working with a very strong marketing plan will bring the limelight to your food truck business. It helps the world to know about you and the things you have to offer to them. You could use several media for this— colorful graphics, and several other interesting images. Working with an international plan for your market is very important in ensuring that your customers get the exact message you need them to get. Here, we will be discussing some tips that would help you;

1. Branding: In a food truck business, it is indeed your brand that sets you different from the rest, so, you might want to spend some time to ensure that you have something fascinating and unique. Here are some of the things that you can employ to get things moving;

- A logo that is very easy to understand.
- Font: A catchy font for the part of your design that should be in form of a text will help draw people to your business.

- Graphics: Decorate your trucks with graphics that are eye-catching enough to draw customers to you and what you sell. So, as you drive your truck around town, people get to know of your business.
- Copy: You could use as many words as possible on your branding medium. Details like the food you cook should not be missing. This factor is also very useful when you make posts on your social media or for your online publications.

2. Website development: You need to ensure that you develop a website for your business. The website will be useful in;
- Showcasing the schedule of your location: Since you don't have any fixed location, your potential customers must know where to reach you. Ensure that you are extremely detailed when giving this information.
- Menu: Once people are captivated by the images and text on your website, they'd go ahead to check out the items on your menu. And trust me,

if they see something they like, they would run to you for more.

- Typical hours and Locations: This is the stage where you let people know how available you are during the week. Include the places you are most likely to work in so that your potential customers can decide if it is a place for them to purchase their lunch or breakfast. Or maybe they'd need to come over during the weekend on a trip to see what you have got.
- Your mission statement: Write something engaging as your mission statement to give people more reasons to buy from you. If you take this seriously, you could go a long way to improve your marketing.
- Pictures of your food: Foods taken with sharp cameras usually come out looking very delicious and attractive. So, you want to ensure that you pay adequate attention to this area.

3. Social media marketing: You might think social media is majorly there for you to chat and advertise your business. But then, it can be a great weapon you can wield when you need to grow

your food truck business. Let us now look at a few ways you can achieve growth;

- Reviews: Reviews are the comments and questions that people drop on your website after accessing your food truck. The way you attend to the questions dropped usually does a lot to help your business grow.

- Two-way communication: By creating polls on the locations your customers desire to be at, you can know what they think of your food items. These details usually work a lot to ensure that you have a steady supply of ideas to work with. You could also get useful tips on how you can run your business.

- Photos: Supplying your customers with images of your menu items comes as a great way of marketing your menu items. Ensure that you post as often as possible—daily, weekly—and when you have special offers. Then, you could tag the photos with very captivating captions.

- Giveaways: You can encourage people to engage your accounts by offering them gift items and cash prizes. This will no doubt draw people to see the things you have to offer on your page. You could also partner up with food bloggers and local magazines to ensure that you get more exposure for your business.

- Allow your customers to do the marketing: You reposting the photos that your customers tagged you in can encourage them to do more. And really, you would be surprised how giving them credit for their contributions can expand your business.

A few social media platforms that you can use to develop your business include;

- Yelp: This platform allows people to rate and review your business. Yelp will encourage your customers to leave reviews for you, and yes, you get to include your images. Then, most importantly, you can let people know of the prices of your menu items here on Yelp.
- Facebook: This is one platform that allows you to engage your customers deeply. Facebook will allow you to create events that your customers can easily add to their calendars. A few of these events could be you planning on feeding hungry

people or something related to that. Facebook will also allow you the chance to view questions that your customers have to ask you.

- Twitter: This is one platform that has shot several businesses to stardom. So, you surely do not want to miss out on the opportunities it can bring to you. Twitter helps you to keep your customers up to date as regards your movements and activities on your food truck. You could also make the world know what values your brand stands for.

- Instagram: Instagram is one platform where you can make the pictures of your item dishes known to the world. So, it is very important to work with the right colors and stories. Then, you should also ensure that you post a lot of pictures on your Instagram story page. To get the best rates of engagement on the app, you should also ensure that you work with the polls, the quizzes, and the questions. You should also ensure that you share and repost images uploaded by your customers to give them credit.

Instagram also allows you to come in contact with the influencers in your city so that you can see if they can help you post a couple of videos and pictures. Influencers usually have several followers and would help you shift the attention of the people to you. In some cases where the influencers have many followers, you might need to pay them though. Instagram reels are another of the ways by which you can generate the needed attention on Instagram. They are short videos that you can fuse music with. They help you to make your interactions with your customers livelier.

- TikTok: This app allows you to shoot your business forward with the aid of videos. It is almost like the reels you make on Instagram. All you need to do is create an account for your food truck, and then, follow influencers in the area to get their attention fixed on you. Some of the strategies you could employ to make this work include;
  - Showing videos of your staff preparing one of your recipes.

- Filming a meal being made from the beginning to the end.
- Shooting videos of events so that you can inform your customers of your catering services.
- Recording the area where you park your truck to let your customers know about your location.

4. Food presentation: Creating appealing presentations of the food you make is another big way by which you can get people to know about your food. Sometimes, when you pay more attention to setting your food items on the plate nicely, you end up getting paid even more. Now, how can you get this strategy done?

- Make use of the right dishware, and cups to make the food look even more appealing. To make your food the major thing that everyone looks out for, you should try working with white containers.
- Clever containers: An example of a clever container is a cup of noodles Styrofoam cup that allows you to serve gourmet ramen.

- Special embellishments: This process involves you adding more flavor, color and texture to your food to make it look more appealing. You could also work with flowers, herbs and spices.

Most of the foods that are sold on a food truck include cupcakes, sliders, tacos. Gyros, lobster rolls, sandwiches, grilled cheese, pizzas, popsicles, etc.

5. A food truck app: Several food applications have been designed today to assist thousands of food truck businesses. Using these applications will help to ensure that your message is passed directly to your target customers. A few of these apps include;
    - Roaming hunger: This food app is used widely in Europe, North America, and China. Here, all you need to do is create an account, and then, include details as regards your locations and patrons. You could also get to get connected to opportunities like events. So, to stay relevant, ensure that you make your customers know of the special offers that you have for them.

- Where's the Food truck Vendor app: This app contains most of the food truck businesses in America. It shares your details with your potential customers, and also, connects your social media to catering opportunities.
- Find your local food truck app: This app allows you to get the attention of potential customers in your region.

6. Location strategies: Before you choose any location for your business, it is important to identify your target customers. So, you need to get in touch with the agents in the society that know when and where there'd be a lot of activity so that you can plan ahead. You also should know that you cannot just park your food truck anywhere you, please. Ensure that you follow the rules and regulations of your city. Some places where you can locate your food truck include;
- Food Truck Parks
- Medical Campuses
- Markets
- College Campuses
- Local Events

- Public Parks
7. Catering: This is one way by which you could use your food truck business to get a steady flow of income. It is also another way you can catch the attention of a few more prospective customers. Catering can be done in events like weddings, conferences, retirement parties, retreats, and graduation parties.

8. Partnerships: Partnerships allow you to merge efforts with local business units and other food trucks so that you can increase your customers. You may never know, but then, the support offered to you by other businesses would indeed go a long way to grow your business. A few of the ideas you could work with here include the following;
   - Food Truck rallies
   - Breweries
   - Movie Theaters
   - Book Stores
   - Farmer's Markets
   - Museums
   - Shopping centers.

9. Merchandising: Merchandising your brand with a logo will encourage your customers to spread the word about you. When doing this though, ensure that you choose something related to what you have to offer. A few of the ideas you can work on include the following;
   - T-shirts
   - Stickers
   - Mugs
   - Keychains
   - Lanyards

These things may seem like the hackneyed stuff that every other business owner does, but indeed, it gives your customers a chance to get you more customers.

The end... almost!

Hey! We've made it to the final chapter of this book, and I hope you've enjoyed it so far.

If you have not done so yet, I would be incredibly thankful if you could take just a minute to leave a quick review on Amazon

Reviews are not easy to come by, and as an independent author with a little marketing budget, I rely on you, my readers, to leave a short review on Amazon.

Even if it is just a sentence or two!

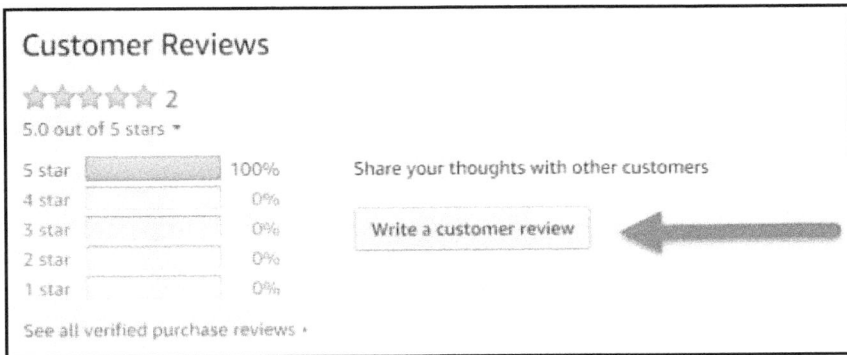

Customer Reviews

★★★★★ 2
5.0 out of 5 stars ▾

5 star		100%
4 star		0%
3 star		0%
2 star		0%
1 star		0%

Share your thoughts with other customers

Write a customer review

See all verified purchase reviews ›

So if you really enjoyed this book, please...

>> Click here to leave a brief review on Amazon.

I truly appreciate your effort to leave your review, as it truly makes a huge difference

Chapter 11

Food Truck Mistakes to Avoid

Now that you know all the necessary prerequisites to own a food trucking business, you should get acquainted with a couple of mistakes that you have to avoid as you begin your food trucking business. What things will you do that could probably ruin things? What rules should you enforce to see that things run smoothly? Here, we will take a look at some of them.

1. Picking a truck with the wrong size: Usually, when you choose a truck that is too small, probably because you plan on cutting costs, you and your employees may end up being cramped all day long in the food truck. And that could affect how you serve your customers. If you also purchase a truck that is too big, you might end up being left with little or no money to operate your business. So, be honest about what you need — space and equipment — to allow yourself to make the necessary plans.

2. Planning your target area inadequately: Several big issues could arise when you do not recognize where your target customers are. So, see to it that you work with a plan that is strong enough to target the areas with your target customers— schools, parks, festivals, etc.

3. Wrong management of staff: You must figure out the exact number of workers you need on your truck and the schedules you need them to work by. To get your staff working at their best, you'd need to see to it that you have enough managerial skills.

4. Working part-time: You have to ensure that you do not just work when you feel like it. Your food truck business requires consecration and hard work to get it to the point you need it to be in. That is why you have to do away with the idea of working only for a few hours. You want to see that you are taking enough time planning out strategies, making recipes, planning out special offers, and all other stuff that would make your customers keep coming back for more.

5. Not paying attention to all the parts of your food truck business: There are several other sides apart

from cooking that you need to pay attention to as you run this business. For example, you want to ensure that your employees are doing their assigned jobs and that the bills are paid. It is also your job to see that the licenses and permits required for your business are gotten or renewed. Lastly, you also need to consider the parking area of your business to get people to come to you.

6. Being inappreciative to your customers: You should always ensure that you offer quality customer service to your customers. Ensure that you offer them delicious meals worth more than their money covers. You would be surprised at how customers can help you spread the name of your business to areas you don't even know of.

7. Keeping your workspace disorganized: Ensure that you keep your working space organized as it will help to keep you and your customer safe, from mechanical and chemical injuries. You also want to ensure that the bills, receipts, and paper works are kept neatly somewhere in your truck.

8. Trying to attend to the needs of everyone: Surely, you could feel like you have the power to see to it that everyone is happy and satisfied. But then,

what that does to you, in the long run, is to get you endlessly frustrated. You could even end up making food of a low quality that will only chase your customers away. Ensure that you always go for food choices that are in one niche to avoid multitasking too much.

9. A bad business plan: A business plan will ensure that you are right on track. It will also let you know how you can plan your finances to know how you should work around situations. For this to work out, you would need to plan out something detailed at the right start.

10. Thinking that you need very little starting capital: Setting up a food truck may not be as expensive as setting up an actual restaurant, but then, you would still need to spend money. You would need to get your equipment ready, clean, and store them. You would also need to get enough money that you can use to cover for licenses and raw materials. In all you do, ensure that you set up very realistic figures when making your calculations.

11. Expecting quick profits: The first thing you need to expect after opening this business is you

regaining all your expenses. After that, you can then classify the rest of your income as profits. So, before you open your business, ensure that you have funds that are just enough to keep your business running, and to get all the raw materials that you need.

12. Settling for cheap equipment: Never should you buy cheap equipment for the sake of making money as that could be very bad for your business. You would end up having food of low quality and that can be very bad for your customers. It could also do a lot to your finances as you would have to spend more money maintaining and buying new ones.

13. Cooking without an official recipe: Having a recipe will help ensure that the taste, texture and manner with which you present a food item remain constant. So, you have to ensure that you do not cancel out the effect of recipes as your customers would keep on coming because they know that they'd get the same delicious food every single time.

Conclusion

The food trucking business was established back in the days, but then it is still a thriving business even in modern times. For this reason, you should brace up well enough and get acquainted with the ins and out to operate and run a successful food trucking business, which is the reason why this book, *The Food Truck Business Book,* was written.

This book sets out virtually all the strategies, and processes to follow when starting your food truck business; so ensure you have fully gained an understanding of all that has been discussed in this book before kickstarting your business; this will ensure your business does not fail like most newbies in this industry.

With this go-to guide, you can be sure of starting on the right note and ending with a great return on your investments, irrespective of the challenges you might encounter, which is typical of every new business startup.

So, with an exact measure of meticulousness in following all that has been discussed, a measure of uniqueness, and of course delectable menus, you are on your way to running a successful food truck business you and every other can be proud of.